Broken Lenses

by

Tequila Rose

DORRANCE
PUBLISHING CO
EST. 1920
PITTSBURGH, PENNSYLVANIA 15238

Dorrance Publishing Co
585 Alpha Drive
Suite 103
Pittsburgh, PA 15238
Visit our website at *www. dorrancebookstore.com*

ISBN: 979-8-8860-4155-2
eISBN: 979-8-8860-4811-7

I would like to thank my dearly loved children, Charles and Alexandria, for not remembering everything. I'd also like to thank my siblings who have heard me speak of creating this work more than a dozen times and for never echoing the sound and thoughts of a parent saying, "I knew you could never do it. I knew you would never accomplish this."

Thank you to my sister Rose for putting that little ditty on social media because it spurred me into greater action.

And thank you to my sister Betty for asking me, "How is the book going?" and making me really think I needed to get back to this work.

Thank you Derry and Marsha, cousins/niece and nephew, who saw life in high school differently and caused me to think that maybe, just maybe, there really were a few good days. I did have a few good, close friends there.

Thank you LH an ML, my life team, for always praying for and listening to me. Again and again and again.

Thank you, most of all, to Pastor TM and his wife E for the hundreds of countless hours of sacrifice, hours of prayer over me, and the hours of training that finally led me to this point. Not all was in vain. And to Pastor JL as he attempted to carry on with spiritual affirmation and counsel after TM retired.

Thanks to the CV-19 virus for giving me more time alone, more time to reflect, more time to study God's Word, and more time for me to try to find ways to be happy, all by myself!!! Now, I am truly done with this virus, as I am sure the rest of the world is too! Pray for a big, God-sized miracle of relief. What a blessing to see all those souls saved and coming to Christ, not dying from despair, disease, or being forced to be alone.

ALL GLORY TO GOD, AND TO HIM ALONE
I GIVE ALL THE PRAISE!

With much love, "Tequila Rose"
Aka: Susan A. Brooke/SAB
And affectionately by my former work team as "Essay."

The Beginning

Not my beginning of life, because it is more like the middle of my story which really has another beginning.

This is the middle of my life. It is the beginning of the healing journey. The path that was chosen by me to finally be taken. And what a path it has proven to be.

In order to get to here from there, I have to give some background. I didn't want to write this as a story of the horrors of an abused child. I wanted something different. This is the story how the healing came to be. So, I have to back up - back to the days of the late 2000s. There was a Bible conference going on at our church. I was assisting in the bindery room one Sunday afternoon when I got a call from my sister. She informed me that my daughter was trying to commit suicide and I needed to go home. I quickly informed the room leader I had to leave. Then I called our children's pastor and asked him to pray. I didn't have real connections to any of the other pastors at that time, even though my daughter and I had been attending church there for a long time, and we were "kissing cousins" to the lead pastor and his wife.

On the drive home I ignorantly called the ex-boyfriend and fought with him until I reached home. I knew he had emotionally abused her. I was so angry with him I could have spit nails. I knew he was the reason she was taking these drastic actions. The city police offered a ride versus the cost-inducing ambulance, and my daughter was taken to the psych ward at a nearby hospital. Because of what she had consumed, she had ruined her potassium levels and was there for five days. During that stint, I had a lot of time for reflection and contemplation. Not one of the people who we had been in a group with at church ever contacted her during that time even though she thought of most of them as second mothers. I missed the rest of the entire Bible conference. But I also knew there was something much deeper going on with my daughter. I was so hard-headed and not yet broken spiritually that I did not know what to do. I thought maybe my spirituality needed a check-up (HA!). An acquaintance of mine once told me that if I ever had "stuff" going on in my life, to go see this certain pastor at the church and he would help me through it in three to four months. WHOA! Three to four months! That sounded like a miracle to me, so I called him. Took me two months after my daughter was released from the hospital to garner the courage to do it, but I finally did.

What you need to know here is that I had had a lot of years of abuse, not only as a child, but as an adult. I had just as many years of shame, if not more, to hide. I didn't want anyone prodding into my past with a poker stick and a micro-lens microscope. However, I set the appointment in December of that year. We met, the first time with his assistant. She told me her story of abuse at the first meeting. Then I met with him again, this time without the assistant, though she was nearby. I didn't really feel like I was getting anywhere with this healing miracle. Then the admin assistant fell ill, and in January of the following year, passed on. Out of courtesy to him and her memory, I waited several weeks, then called to resume the appointments. Those first few meetings after that turned into hours of counseling! I think I may have been a diversion from his pain of loss. I would feel like I was finally getting somewhere. And, of course, he had to leave and go home. He did have a family. I would complain that he couldn't leave me like that, so he'd tell me to come back another day that week. I would talk for another several hours. I couldn't wait for meetings with this counseling pastor each week. I was always in anticipation and anxiety of what I would end up saying while there and how he would respond or what he would say.

He asked lots of questions at first and very patiently explained about differences in a good vs. bad God-view and the ways of the world. To say that this man embodied the face of God to me is putting it mildly. After months of crying on his desk, I finally broke down and started relaying everything from the past. After nine long and exhausting months, I finally gave in and forgave everyone of every past hurt and pain. At least I thought I did. I cried and cried, and some days he wept with me. I know now that HE (God) wept with me. I cannot tell you how many times the pastor did, but I know he did. He doesn't know that I know, but if he ever reads this, he will.

That response, in and of itself, was so touching to me, but I still couldn't believe in love. Nor did I believe in trust. But week after week, month after month, he'd tell me that he loved me and showed me the compassion of a Godly man. He showed me how much my God-view was skewed by my past. About a year later, when I still couldn't understand the unconditional Love of God shown to others through His people, he brought in a couple that I dearly admired and loved. They also attempted to show me compassion and unconditional love. Too many years of abuse could not be wiped away by a few sessions of counseling. That was all impacted by the fact that after several months I felt like I could no longer hold on to my own faith. I asked this dear man to hold it for me. Not that I didn't believe in God or Jesus Christ anymore, but I did not feel like I still believed in my faith for myself. I am not sure I am making sense here, but I hope and pray that I am.

Almost all parents damage their children. This includes guardians, grandparents as parents, aunts and uncles as parents; anyone filling the parental role. It cannot be helped. Youth, like expensive glass, absorbs the prints of its handlers. Some people smudge, others crack, a few shatter…childhoods completely broken into jagged little pieces. Beyond repair. At the beginning the damage was one of perverted sexual abuse. An abuse no child should ever have to endure. Then the abuse turned into an even uglier form from a different parent as neglect. Later it moved into lashings, beatings, whacking, and screaming profanities. This was the second damage: the damage of violence.*

Silence becomes the escape, but silence is only a refuge. The thoughts still haunt you.*

Parents rarely let go of their children, so the children let go of them. They move away, they move on. The moments that used to define them - looks of disapproval (you know that Mom's eye look?) or a nod of the head by a parent start to cover over by their own moments of accomplishments. It is not until much later that the child understands that their stories sit on top of their parents' stories, and their lives are like water beneath them. In the middle of a big war, you go looking for something to believe in - something, no matter how big or how small, to hold it all together.*

Is it true that fairness does not govern life and death? If it is, then no good person would ever die young. No life would be a waste. The only waste is the time we spend thinking we are alone. Sacrifice becomes a part of life. No sacrifice is too small. We all make sacrifices. But some of us were angry over those sacrifices. We keep thinking about all that was lost. What if we redirect our thinking and think about all that was gained or all that we could be grateful for? I think maybe that's what heaven will be for. You get to make sense of all your yesterdays.*

I'm praying and hoping that parts of this book will be taken with a note of irony, as a paradox. According to the world's dictionaries, the word means "a statement that is seemingly contradictory or opposed to common sense, and yet, perhaps, is true." What basically seems silly to the world will be the very thing that will usher in the power of God. The world's way of doing things will be seemingly backwards. Up will be down. Left will be right. Wrong will be right. Gaining is losing. Losing is gaining. Last is first. And living will be dying. Anything ordinary will seem unordinary. It is never hard to act ordinary if you feel ordinary, and the paleness of your surrender becomes the color of your days. And then nothing is contradictory or opposing to common sense. I grew up not knowing common sense. My life was a series of paradoxes, and yet, all too true."

I can state that there were many days of tears. Not false tears. For false tears are those meant only for oneself. They were tears that were words from the heart that could not be spoken, coming from a life whose heart was broken. Not just broken but shattered. Into a million billion tiny pieces, too small to find and use to repair. My only saving grace in all these years was that I could NOT, no matter what I did in my life, I could not OUT SIN God's grace. I pray for forgiveness over what you may read or interpret into these poems of my beginning journey. To quote an often-stated line from the TV show, *800 Words*: "Sometimes you have to blow things up to clear the air and start over again."* *And from the movie *Touched by Romance*: "Creating art is discovering your inner self; creating art is the purest form of self-improvement and realization." I had to realize through many, many years of writing and languishing over the creation of this work, that to step towards my destiny, I had to step away from my security, my comfort zone. I have to learn to hear and take rejections with a grain of salt. Rejection. Who needs it? Especially when your whole life has felt like a big series of rejections. But today, I DARE TO DREAM! My random thoughts and words in script are on this page and the pages following. I have written many more words of poetry; however, they are lost in journals long since thrown away. I couldn't dare let my children see my crazed self then. Or they were written in my mind while I was driving down the road, heading somewhere, anywhere but here, and they were meant for only God to hear.

As you will undoubtedly read and comprehend, I am neither a proficient nor an eloquent speaker. I am not overeducated in the literary sense. I barely survived high school and those first two semesters of college. Although college studies were easier for me, I still could not pass that darn reading and writing exam. Pardon my French, but who the hell cares if you can pass a reading or writing exam if what you write is palatable and makes sense to others?

If one soul is saved from a destiny of hell, then this attempt at writing was all worth it.

My final words for now are that silence in and of itself is the most BASIC and INTIMATE form of humility. STOP TALKING just to be heard! And, if you are a child of God, get healing in your life now, for the shame of your life cannot be seen in the light of the Son.

x ~ Tequila Rose

Dark Times

"The Darkness Before"

Oh, these dark and dreary thoughts
My world's so full of gloom
They swirl and tumble, churning in my mind
Speak of impending doom;
To be freed; to feel; once without despair
Would be all I ask for; if I'd even dare
So constant, so agonizing, my body only feels pain
Going down, growing deeper, into the depths again
No insight, no relief, no peace, nowhere to turn;
Stuck with words, these thoughts, my brain feels so burned;
My eyes are blurred, I no longer see;
What can remove these thoughts inside, unfree;
What can I do, who'll help me see
How to turn off these thoughts consuming me;
I scream in my head, but who can hear?
Free me, free me!! I shed one lonely tear.

SA Brooke
June 2010

What Life?

You stole, you stole my life from me
Now only God can give it back and set me free;
You took my soul, I was abhorred
Only God can take and with love restore;
My life I've lived in shambles, shame and fear
Kept REAL life at bay, no one comes near
 How did you hurt a child so?
The things you did, you stooped so low;
Unprotected and left for wolves in town
Hunted and ridiculed, left all alone.
What was this child, so lost, to do?
Couldn't place trust in people like you.
Had to learn to run, to hide from the chase
My life became a lie, abased;
With none to love, so cold, so cold
My heart turned to stone, a lie to hold
Lies became the life I knew
My heart now had turned to blue;
No heat to warm it, no true love found
Hearts are shattered, stomped to the ground;
Got to find someone, a spark, a light
Show me real love, hold on, hold me tight;
Don't let me go, till what I know
Is God's real love, through you it'll grow;
Do I dare? Do I dare to believe?
can't be hurt no more, stomped on, made to grieve.
My faith's too small, it needs to grow

Show me the truth, the way I don't know;
Enter the light, give me the love
Exemplify the gift sent from heaven above.

SA Brooke
July 10, 2010

To Believe

Fragmented pieces of my mind
Have nowhere to go
Fragmented pieces of my heart
Have taken me low
To love, to live, to grow, to believe;
All foreign to me, is it something to grieve?
Go who, what, where, why and how;
Do I get from this place to the here and now?
I'm so tired of the pieces of my heart
Broken, shattered, and torn apart.
Shellshocked and worn,
TRAUMA BE DAMNED!
I WANT TO BELIEVE, I want to stand!!!
Wholly complete, with no mask on my face
I want to work out my faith, salvation in place.
HOW DO I GET THERE? What do I do?
Tell me PLEASE GOD, I am begging you!!!

SA Brooke
April 18, 2011

This Far for a Reason

Though this may not be the season
Of my life that shows I'm lovingly pleasin'
I've come this far for a reason.

The path was long, dark, and full of pain
Through many heartaches filled with rain
I've come this far for a reason.

To choose a better path, a life
God's righteousness instead of strife;
I've come this way for a reason.

The doubts still come and show their face
But the fear I've had is being replaced,
I've come this far for a reason.

Forgiveness given gives life from above
Forgiveness gotten shows a life of love.
I've come this far for a reason.

I'm on this path called righteous living
This path can show the love being given
I've come this far for a reason.

No selfish cries as hurts unfold
We all got pains, some yet untold,
I've come this far for a reason.

Be of it, not in it, that's not the world
Keep on keeping on, life's righteous ways unfurled.
I've come this far for a reason.

Though this is not yet the season
My life begins to show righteous pleasin'.
I've come this far for a reason.

I've faced some demons
Not all in my mind
Some who said, "I'm God's people"
But who were really mean and unkind.
I've come this far for a reason.

Love given is love restored
The heart is opening, waiting for more
The broken pieces once shattered and torn
The life is healing, being reborn.

SA Brooke
March 1, 2011

The Silence of Dreams

What were the dreams of long ago?
Still holding to it; or are you letting go?
Dreams have to die to be fulfilled
But wait! My life was silenced, was stilled,
Dreams didn't live there
No thoughts of other love
My mind was silenced
Filled with other stuff, plugged.

Have to forgive, repent, release them, let go
Can't live your life if you don't grow
Choose the path, the way, you'll see
Life's little changes begin new memories.

Capacity for hurts, now being shed
Open the way for a life to be led
By the God of all wonders
His greatest glory to share
No more silent dreams in your mind
His way opened for his love, feel how he cares.

The burdens that once riddled and crippled your heart
Are being released, it's new start
With the God of all wonders
His greatest joy is now spilled
Into a heart with capacity for love to be filled.

SA Brooke
March 1, 2011

The Me Who I Thought I Was

Hello, she said
What's your name? they asked
Oh, people usually call me by my given name, she said
What's that? they asked

Susan, she said, Susanna in the Bible. It means lily, grace, and
beauty,
According to Biblical definitions.
Hmmmm, kinds of seems appropriate, they said
Not if you know the real me, she said

What's different? they asked
The ME who I think the real ME is does not know who the real
ME is, she said
Can you help us understand? they asked.

I can't even begin to explain because I don't even know who the other
part(s) of me are, she said. I pulled from deep within myself at coun-
seling and found that I am a disassociated personality; that I am of at
least one, maybe more, other personalities, but I cannot recall any of
them. I cannot recall a time when any of them came out, so I don't
even know if the me I think I am today is the real me. Who was it ex-
actly that emerged as the victorious one after all the trauma? The me
who I think I am is a believer, but does that mean that all the other
hidden parts of me are also believers?

Who AM I God? she cried. Who am I really? I always said I had a
defragmented personality! I guess my "all of me" knew that, but the
exterior one won't let the other personalities be as they were. She (or

he pretending to be a she) has led me (us?) to believe she had unified them. Maybe it's the devil's reign over her other parts that has led her to believe they have been unified?

SA Brooke
October 22, 2011

(This is an example of the defragmented thoughts abuse survivors have.)

What are those words that you have spoken?
By your thoughts they have been chosen.
Words of such insanity -
Do you really need such profanity?
Words should be chosen, tender and fair;
Spoken with much great grace and care.
Do you mean to hurt, to ridicule;
To tear into another's hearts fuel?
To burn there till all is ash
To ignore, let lie, be unabashed?
The wound is so much deeper
Cuts through like a bow
It can't be much cheaper
Than when you stooped so low.
A thought to ponder
While you choose to disdain
You could lose the one at which
You choose to yell your profanes.
Daily, death and dying is all around us
Was it really worth making all that fuss?

SA Brooke
2/28/2012

Lighter Lenses

Healing Ways

Who is that man
With kindly face;
What can you see;
What's pictured?
 Is that "grace"?

He looks on me
With eyes of truth;
I'm Words unspoken, I've no emotions
And yet, He sees right through.

How does he know,
What's in my eyes;
Brokenness, wearied
Empty from lies?

Reflecting pools of the soul
Woundedness was not the goal;
Find a way to bring back the light
Find a way to diminish the night.

Grace, hmm, what? Is that here?
Would I know grace, staring at me, while I in fear,
A Soul so lost, I can't bear
To look back, to see what's there?

I took the dare, I began to walk
A journey on a path; I begin to talk;

Break free, little one, bare your soul
The God above, he wants you whole.

Wants to show me the love, the light, his grace
All by that man's kindly embrace.
With eyes showing love, not untrue or fake,
He knows what I need is on that man's face.

S.A. Brooke
2/29/12

Healing Heart

A child caught
Between love and hate;
Is that what love's
Supposed to propagate?
In their prison
Called their life;
They've woven a snare
Fraught with strife.
The child, afraid,
Nowhere to turn
Has learned to be
Aware, to discern
That this is not
What her life should be;
Alone, learning to distrust
Her life encompassing loss
Because of an insatiable lust
Direction skewed
Nowhere to turn
Life needs to be renewed
But, afraid she'll again be burned
Life stops, she's caught unawares
Their actions have her in the enemies snares
Must be a way, some light
Has to be a path
Out of this constant fight
To survive daily in this swath
Not herself, she's become

Some former shadow
Of what other's see her as
So far below
What God designed, deigned
Not what has been feigned
Burnt, frosted, used, lost, no joy
She turns in one last chance
To put her life in the hands
Of one who holds a key
To what will be the last dance
Alone, unknown, unloved, no solution
Is turned to life with resolution;
No longer a heart of stone
No longer feeling all alone
Healings fingers have begun
To touch that heart, unable to love
And trust, brings victory through the blood
Of one who teaches us to overcome.
Won't give up this fight
The enemy will have to take flight
I will overcome; I will overcome.
You can beat my head against
That constant door of fear
But I will rest in Abba's arms
As he gives me a path that's clear
For today is all I need to
Put one foot in front of the other
And make a move to be
Held in high esteem, like my brothers
And sisters in Christ who have
Chosen the path of slave

To a love, Sight unseen
Yet able to be believed.

S.A. Brooke
March 17, 2012

He Won't Let It Go

Why won't he leave me alone?
This thing called Satan mocking on his mock throne.
He knows I'm vulnerable, still in shock;
Fear, doubt, and anguish, used to be a constant frock.
I haven't attained the place of trust;
Going backwards again, I feel such loss.
Is what I desire really so much more;
Than what's behind the seemingly elusive door?
Why do I struggle, strive, and shove;
Wanting to believe in God's great love?
He plays with my mind, my thoughts, my words;
I put it asunder, with my God's Word.
Still he pokes, he prods, he announces in vain;
You'll never be over this, there's too much pain.
You know what you've done! The accuser will scream;
You can't have any of what you once dreamed.
You gave up their life, you stunted their growth;
Now you have to pay for it, he continually boasts.
Forgiveness, he snarls, must be accepted;
And you are in development arrested.
You're far too immature to be
Able to attain maturity.
You can't forgive yourself, you've hurt so many;
Though not really your fault, still you tasted the candy.
Living daily with the constant reminders;
You see their pain, unable to go beyond the hinder
Parts of their life. Dysfunction, unbelief in their eyes;
Wondering what's to become of their lost lives.

This quandary, dilemma, my constant foes;
this is why I write this prose.

SA Brooke
4/24/12

Something to Gain

Thought surely by now, I'd be rid of this pain
But…here I am, back here again.

Don't be mad, child, it's a needed thing
And don't you act like it's just nothing;

I need you to know it's there for s reason,
It may be a short or a very long season.

I need you to know so you'll think of me,
If I don't send reminders, you'll forget and I'll be
Like a ship at sea, adrift, no one aboard
Waiting, just waiting, for you to come back from the shore.

If I let you forget, take away the pain
You'll forget about me, I've nothing to gain.

I want your thoughts, your words, sent above
To show you remember, you care, you love
Me, this one who first endured all the pain
I took it from you, so you'd have something to gain.

SA Brooke
4/26/12

SON
Shining in Darkness

Released

I'm being freed, oh yes,
From this pit of Hell.
Known it most my life,
Known it all too well.

Darkness, shadows, gut-wrenching pain
Waiting for the worst, always living in the rain.
Moments of laughter could not dispel,
The hold on my heart, I could not quell.

Couldn't hear, couldn't feel, couldn't see
His holding on would set me free.
Though times were ugly, not meant to be shared;
Someone took the innocence, how did they dare?

All is not lost, child, His voice finally heard
Through all your pain, whispered forgiveness is the word,
You must speak it, to heal it, and not just for the end,
What matters is you and not all of them.
What matters is you, in the here and now,
What matters is you, and those tears on your brow.
Release them and you from the bondage they hold
Release them and you'll find more than the cold
Stares of unknowing, disbelieving eyes
All thinking you're telling a big pack of lies.

Was it meant for the purpose of the greater good
This pain you endured, like I said it would.

What you do each day, living with me
Inside of you, matters, has purpose, sets you free.

It's Me, your true Papa, the Spirit, your Brother
We're what matters, and there's none other.
None who can live in you, work with you, be servant and friend,
None who can feel, see, hear all your pain till the end.

I am the Living One, giver of life.
I watched and felt every bit of your strife.
The struggles, the sobs, torn from your heart,
I felt it all with you, twas the hardest part.

Choices were made, I watched your fears,
Used of a freedom bought with a son's life and tears.
I cannot rule the choices they made, or chaos ensued;
The earth was ensnared, couldn't be subdued.

Life has to be lived in the fashion it is
For the future to unfold, to bring about bliss.
Is it beautiful for a life to be used, abused, and taken;
Not by my love, but has theirs also been shaken?

They were twisted sometime in their path too
Which they lived out in their actions towards you.
Not meant to be, I had to let them be and do,
Those choices they made when they hurt you.

The purpose still is for the greater good,
The price you paid was something you should
Embrace. Hold on to your thoughts, but not in your heart;
Forgiveness of everyone can make the right start.

It's time to let it all go now, your worst was your best;
Time to live only through us and our love and let US do the rest.
You're healing; find love, live those dreams till that hope
Has been realized and you're basking in the glory of heaven above.

S A Brooke
4/28/12

I Can't Seem to Hear You Tonight

I want you to speak to me through these words tonight
But I am having trouble putting the thoughts together, trying to be
polite;
To make a meaningful sentence, so profound and true,
Is currently a lot easier said than done for me, not for you.

Maybe I should just let the words come from what's within
Caring naught if it makes me look black as sin;
I am distressed, you know this, Papa.

I need a place, not out on the road proper;
Now, perhaps, my child will come too
With animals, so we'll need more room;
You KNOW without a doubt that I am scared;
Scared that there's nothing going to work out.
I thought I had a place when Sean wanted to buy
Places to rent, I should have known better, it was too good, pie in sky;
You know, Papa, how I struggle with these things in my mind.
I'm not good enough for great fortune to find;
Please, PAPA, please, let someone call me with an offer,
A rent affordable, a place that's sunny, open, and roomy,
A place that holds all of us, without us getting gloomy;
A place for entertaining old friends, new friends, family, and more
Whoever you bring into our lives, let us put into the store
House of our hearts and minds; willing servants to your
Thoughts, ways and your way of being kind. Being a Jesus to the
friend and the foe
Though we know how hard loving the foe unfolds
Which brings me to the owners of this place

Who want to stomp on me with their ugly ungrace;
Such two-faced liars and cheats, who think they can
Win over your ways, your knowledge, your grace.
Protect me from them, Papa Dear;
Stay close to me when I respond in their ear.
The truth as it is, the one they won't provide;
But truth, as it is, shall always abide.
Give me peace and direct my path, my feet, my mind
And let me know the place we're to move, the place to find.
Soon and very soon, Dear Papa, to keep me from making
A stupid, unintelligent, emotional decision, a mistake, where l get taken.
Again!

SA Brooke
7/11/12

Now What?

What's going on in their hearts tonight?
Are their minds making choices that may not be right?
Are they making choices only themselves to fill
With things they want, with no regard to others, still?
Are they selling their souls to the devil, so to speak
To think they're finding a happiness that's just as bleak?
Having to lie, to cheat others, taking actions hateful and dark,
To attempt to assuage themselves with what is their lark;
How many more things will be in my head,
Spinning around dizzying me making me crazy instead
Of keeping the silence and easygoing pace,
I'd gotten when I finally realized your grace.
Take me back to that place, please Papa, please
I'm begging you NOW, I need a treatise!
I want to beg that the ones who are trying to hurt me
Be hurt even more, feel excruciating pain of loss,
And find they can hardly breathe!
The ones have turned their backs on you
In favor of "love" that's not known to be true.
As well as having a "man" and his money
All for the sake of calling him 'honey.'
But I know it is wrong to try to exact revenge
You'll take care of it all and move me past it
With things they'll never know, may even make cringe.
What a glorious victory that would be, I'd be laughing;
But here I go again, wanting to watch them lose and be writhing
In more pain than what they have exacted upon me
Lord Jesus, HELP ME; I want to remain free!

S A Brooke
7/11/12

Relationships and life for 2012

This is exactly right about me…

This has been going on for so many years now, it's starting to feel like the status quo. You've certainly been to hell and back so often in recent times that you've grown accustomed to picking up the pieces and starting over. The redeeming factor of this intense transit is that each time you go through a personal cataclysm, you emerge that much stronger. Your ability to regenerate is astonishing at this point. You've weeded out the toxic relationship patterns and - more importantly - the negative people from your life. When it comes to love, you are the Phoenix!

Poetry's Other Thoughts

The Second Law of Thermodynamics
"A closed system becomes more and more chaotic over time."

Tears
Tears are words from the heart that can't be spoken;
Coming from a life of one whose heart was broken.

Open the door to your heart, let yourself out.

False tears are selfish tears meant only for yourself.

SA Brooke
4/24/15
11:44 PM

Heaven's Gate

Alone at Heaven's gate I stand
Not waiting on my Savior's hand
His hand I took when I was young
A new song in my heart was begun
But I won't be here alone for long.
God's opened the gate, here comes the throng!
Rejoicing, hugging, laughing we sing,
Not songs of sorrow, for I've a new life to begin.
A life in heaven with my Father so dear,
Raise your glasses high; don't you dare cry;
Dance with me and give a Big Cheer!

S A Brooke
4/24/15
11:44 PM

Who's Plan?

Looking around, there's an aura of despair,
Our lives fastidiously moving to disrepair.
The enemy's attacks pulling like moths to a flame,
Speaking lies of greatness without any shame.
Drawing deeper to anxiety and fear
Thoughts unravel, become unclear.
Choices made fit only my desires
No concern for playing with fire.
Desperately holding to "I want things my way"
We push God out, far and away
Now there's no hope, the future is bleak,
What's left? Nothing!
Enemy's status on you? Complete!!!

SA Brooke
March 20, 2016

While Healing Begins

Daily, each moment living with the fear
How long on my knees, my face, till it's clear?
I need your deliverance, salvation today.
Why, God, do you seem so far away?

How do I trust, find peace in your rest?
Why can't I be the one who's extremely blessed?
Sweet relief from these pressures and more,
I feel like I'm stuck, only wading the shore.

I want to be moved from here to there
Show me your ways, your steps, your fare.
Patience, my child, your time's coming near,
Wait for the sounds of silence and you'll hear
I've got something greater for you, my Dear.

SA Brooke
March 20, 2016

Open the Door of Your Heart

Open the door of your heart
And let your wounded self out.
There's parts broken on tracks inside
They need to travel a different route.
On towards the healing,
Go towards the Sun.
They may become jumbled
But never undone.
The healing will wear you down
The route taken may cause you to frown.
The traffic in your mind
Can cause great unrest.
The path you're journeying on
Could lead to your best!
The best of you, you will ever be
Sojourned with healing that sets you free.
You've been so closed
You think all is a chore.
Not meant for you,
Nothing is yours.
Not true, open up to receive, to feel
All can be yours, just lay back the peels.
Slowly awakening, the part needing to heal.
To experience, to feel his love,
Open it up with our Father's help from above.
So much more can be yours, don't be afraid.
I've got you, my darling, from here,
Till it's time for your life you'll trade.

From this old world into heavens above
My love is enough, open for love.

SA Brooke
5/29/16

Passing the Torch

Sadness fell, yet excitement cannot be mocked
As the end of a long era begins;
A Pastor well loved, passing the torch of shepherding the flocks;
A new Pastor, not yet regarded, willingly receives the torch, the
church gets the win.

One man's great legacy around the world
Is taken not lightly by the other
So many lives, the shepherding unfurled
God's spoken choice, becomes our brother.

"What happens now?" the flock has asked;
As the leaders prepare the new way;
The new Pastor's life is now greatly tasked;
God says, "Let me be the leader, if I may?"

The church leaders have spoken
And their hands were laid;
Upon the ones chosen
As the congregation prayed.

New Pastor, you are given the greatest charge,
To care for this flock, some still yet unknown;
With such big shoes to fill, this flock is large,
Reaches from here to around the world, as our old Pastor's legacy
was grown.

We'll pray for you both as the new legacy's begun,
Your wife and family we'll embrace in the fold;

God's word that was spoken through the light of His Son;
Will be shared with the flock, His purpose he's ready to unmold.

SA Brooke
Aug 25, 2017

Open the Door of Your Heart

Open the door of your heart
And let your wounded self out.
There's parts broken on tracks inside
They need to travel a different route.
On towards the healing,
Go towards the Sun.
They may become jumbled
But never undone.
The healing will wear you down
The route taken may cause you to frown.
The traffic in your mind
Can cause great unrest.
The path you're journeying on
Could lead to your best!
The best of you, you will ever be
Sojourned with healing that sets you free.
You've been so closed
You think all is a chore.
Not meant for you,
Nothing is yours.
Not true, open up to receive, to feel
All can be yours, just lay back the peels.
Slowly awakening, the part needing to heal.
To experience, to feel his love,
Open it up with our Father's help from above.
So much more can be yours, don't be afraid.
I've got you, my darling, from here,
Till it's time for your life you'll trade.

From this old world into heavens above
My love is enough, open for love.

SA Brooke
5/29/16

Who Will I Hear?

When I take that step into the car
To go where? Tomorrow, or how FAR?
I wonder who I'll hear the most;
The sounds in my head or God's Spirit, The Holy Ghost?
I know these thoughts that run through my mind
again and again with no thought to the time
It may be morning, noon, or night
Or wee little hours while I'm having a fright;
This trip is for healing, for processing more pain
That's one of the things that I want to gain
Put my healing, my feelings, my thoughts, my poems to you.
Bind it up softly, so others' healing begins
Just knowing that someone else has been
The place you're walking will help them to mend.
This journey is more about what it takes to start healing
Than telling the woeful take of one's lost life and feelings.
It is just the beginning to the new end
With bits of wisdom given for the soul to tend.
To their own hearts and lives and souls
To begin to end their own lives of woes.
Live life freely, with no guilt, no hiding, no shame
And give back to those who have a lot to gain.
Life lived in Christ, the Father, all three
Nothing compares to the glory in thee!

SA Brooke
5/21/15

Remember?

Do you recall what I recall?
Are your memories in sync with mine?
Hold fast to what you believe you trust,
While I'll hold fast to mine.
Memories of past lives lived
Come rushing back
As we reminisce and share
What lurks behind those memories? Should we even care?
Or would we even dare to let go of what we thought was mine?
To be held in concert with what you believed about that time?
Memories, no longer the same
Fused by ideals, life, even shame,
Not your memories, only mine.
Listening you share yours, somewhat sublime;
Idealistic, do not mesh or rhyme
Different, and yet the same?
Can we recall without the blame?
My thoughts, without merit, slain.

S A Brooke
10/4/15

In the Middle of Nowhere

Leaves dance in the aisles of the street
While the wind whistles an indescribable tune
Under the umbrella of a bright blue canopy
Where white whisps float up high,
And suddenly the silence is broken
By the sounds of people rushing by,
Yet going nowhere.

SA Brooke
10/11/15
3:15PM (Arthur, IL)

The Silence

Silence? Where? When?
It should be; except
This sleepy little town no longer sleeps.
The roads, too busy
Are swept with cars,
The buggies pulled by horses
Swoosh, swoosh, clip, clop
The sound of a train's horn blows.
This was once my favorite town,
My favorite sleepy little town;
Sunday's naps now interrupted,
Go, go, go; no longer do we just sit and wonder;
No time to just think and ponder.
Go, go, get on with life,
It calls you from your dreams.

SA Brooke
10/11/15
3:35 PM (Arthur, IL)

What Hurts?

The hurts I feel
Were never meant for me
Jesus bore them all
When he died for me.
The scars I carry
Never meant to be.
Jesus took all the scars
When he died on that tree.

SA Brooke
December 27, 2018

Peace Interrupted

Shimmering and pristine, the water is flowing by
The lone call of the red bird flying by
The stillness pervades the quietness of the day
Till the fighter jet streaming by goes away
Quiet pervades, sun shines, warmer still
The bluebird breaks the silence with its trill
Peace interrupted, the day moves forth
Noise pervades the quiet, with little effort
Once again, the quiet breaks free
Waiting for you, waiting for me.

01/18/2019
Susan A Brooke

Rain

Rain once so violently fell
Came swooping down, not in one spell
Taking life's innocence, a small girl cried
The taking didn't end, even though she tried.
Rains continued, the young girl grew,
But life's hard knocks were hardly through,
Raining in torrents, storms abound
The girl survived each as it came round,
Not sure where she was to land
She put her life into God's hand.
Older now, a bit wiser to be sure,
She understood God's plan was her allure.
Rains fall quieter in her life now
Healing rains have taken a bow.
It wasn't easy, the storms really brewed
Her life without Jesus was really skewed.
Step by step in the storms of life
God taught her quietness, life without strife.
Stillness reigns like the morning dew,
God shed his light; his love accepted anew.

S A Brooke
2019

Silence Becomes the Night

The boom and bangs with noise unfurled,
Were joyously made with rockets hurled;
Now midnight approached
With ne'er a streak of light
Suddenly booms and bangs quietly fade
Into the fog of night
Silence, deafening, where once extreme
Noise was heard,
Sleep escapes me now,
No noise to comfort my world.

SA Brooke
July 4, 2019

Sometimes

Sometimes your voice doesn't need
To be the loudest one in the room to be heard;
Music from the soul is sung from your heart.

SA Brooke
July 15, 2019

Unwanted

I didn't understand
I couldn't see all the hate You had for me.
Now, I'm breakin' through. Now, I can see,
You didn't want the baby girl,
The baby girl, me.
A baby boy was more your choice
But I was what God sent instead.
How could you love what you didn't want?
Can't reconcile your heart, only your head.

Susan A Brooke
January 2, 2020

Life Story

Sanity's fleeting; with everything, I fought!
Sanity's fleeting, over all t'was wrought.
Tensions high, both felt and heard
Not your punching bag, by fist or by word.
Punishments given, your fault, your doom.
Go hide your face from me, in corner of room.
Words hurled, their origins unknown,
Words hurts, no understanding, ah, but the Tone!
Ugliness prevailed, day through night,
Young girl feels jailed, too scared to fight.
Mommy, Mommy, why'd you treat me so?
I can't understand, your blows are so low.
What did I do? l was born of your seed
Your accusations so strong, part of your creed.
No credibility, the girl since grown,
Nowhere to go, to be…she moans.
How do you escape a fate so drear?
By time with a neighbor, 'tis surely clear.
Recall and recoils of time gone by
Must leave this hell, before someone dies.
All hell's broke loose; home, bus, church, and school,
All patrons adding their own little screws.
Treat this girl any way you please,
Her life's a wreck, there's no life to appease.
A short fleeting moment comes, she's still forlorn.
Sanity's briefly restored, a hero was born.
Never forget him, the one who defined
That long term bullying's not considered kind.
The girl now's in shock, a few admonishing words spoken,

The weight lifted here now, a long spell has been broken.
Lacking her own strength, unknown how to fight.
Home's still bad, though school's roughness took flight.
Now learning, no baby girls wanted, says the head
How do you reconcile that with constant dread?
So clearly, slowly, the languishing pain makes sense;
Hurt her, she'll die, no one cares, makes life tense.
Get her Out! the mom screams, Get Away! Disrupting bitch!
Mom wants her own life, and the girl's won't be rich.
Mommy, Mommy, why did you treat me so?
I can't understand, your blows are so low.
Punishments taken as the years fall through
Punishments rendered, it's all on you.
Words stinging, hurting, play 'round the mind.
What's left of this life for this girl to find?
Years of dumping, unknown reactions and more
Left this one's life seeking, searching for more.
Too many years till one person was found
Who heard, who listened, helps her find solid ground.
He embodies the Christ he expounds on and then,
Teaches the love of the One, it's not just a trend.
Living life, the best way known,
Years fly by, like the eagle's flown.
Round and round the attempt is made.
Life is fleeing, no permanence played.
It's not figured out yet, God's life a better bet now.
Just trust me, just love me, your purpose I'll show how.
Years wasted! Never to be returned;
All due to the lies of the life I learned
Now cannot be made up for with one good turn.
Except!!! Through Jesus, the giver of life and sun
Forgave them All, so new lives begun.

How do I stand in Christ's stead?
Wholeheartedly agree to do as he's said?
Forgive them as I, though they knew what they'd done.
Forgive them too, I can't Outshine the Son.
Thankful now to share what little I know,
Moving forward, I add life to those who choose to grow.

S A Brooke
Jan 2, 2020

Poetry Thoughts

What's in my mind?
You cannot tell.
Sometimes I write
For God alone to dwell
On what's in my heart
And thought's today
Words you will not see
And will never slay

Words and thoughts so profound
I wished I had written them down
Alas those poems He's saving for me
Quietly kept in His book with no key
One day He'll release all the words written in prose
The pain, the tears, the love like a rose.
Written between the pages of my mind
He's kept them all bound, and one day I'll find
The peace that comes from knowing he heard
And took the time to remember each and every word.

January 2020
Susan A Brooke

Clouds

Clouds floating, gray, swimming, through blue skies;
Dark, foreboding, telling tales of future times;
White, fluffy, see what is there?
A dino, a flower, a horse, a cuddly teddy bear;
Moving slow, lazy days viewing;
Faster now, a storm's a-brewing;
Twisting, gnarly, strong, a blowing wind
Brings cool, cold, or hot air in;
Gathering droplets, dropping rain;
Flowy snows brings icy plains;
Clouds drifting, freeing hazy mind's eye,
Going nowhere, going everywhere, fly away,
Comes back, seen anew, by another's day try,
Fluffy, bleak, black as night, gone again by the by.

January 2020
Susan A Brooke

Forgiveness

Forgiving you, your scoundrel ways,
Means I've let go of holds meant to make me stay
Bound to you with fetters and moss
But I'm cutting the ties, it's now your loss!

SA Brooke
Jan 2020

A Sunny Day

A day to smile
A day to relax
A day with sunshine warm on our backs,

See the sun shining?
See those in motion?
A sun-shiny day
Is like taking spring's potion.

Laughing, dancing, running,
Picnicking, playing, and more,
Sun-shiny days are made
For love and lovers galore.

January 2020
Susan A Brooke

Gratitude

Be thankful, they say, for every little thing in life.
Be thankful, they say, but depression brings strife.
Winter is depressive, dark, bleak, gray, no sun.
Stuck in the house, weather's so bad, there's no place to run.

So what's to be thankful for when you're stuck and alone?
Well, I guess I can be grateful for lights and warmth, TV and phone.
Food in the house, cat's playing 'round.
Books to read, music to play, a few things I found.

I guess there's always something to be thankful for.
I'm a child of God, maybe sick, but there's more,
Eternity promised, loved unconditionally,
Set in the place of heirship, His life set me free.

January 2020
Susan A Brooke

Romance

What a Joke!
Made up by people;
I call them Blokes!

January 2020
Susan A Brooke

Paths Forged

On the path forged for me, I got lost.
Couldn't find my way, didn't count the cost;
Years stolen and left with no life to show.
Living in survival mode, strife was below.
The path was fraught with snakes and storms galore
Winding round my mind, ever biting for more.
Looking for a glimmer of hope to see;
Wandering, darkness falling, unable to free.
Will I find the path forged once again
Or will I be stagnant stuck in dark rains?
Wait! Slowly, the dark storms rise
On the path, the snakes cannot devise
A plan to keep the lost one from siege.
A brighter light shines, chasing them off with ease.

Susan A Brooke
January 2020

Expectations

Are you who people think you are?
Though they don't really know you, but from afar?

Do their thoughts really matter?
Their words, that they splatter
Everywhere for the world to hear?
What they don't really know but speak from fear?

Suppositions and motives cross through their mind
And afraid of the truth, they speak what they find.
They think their findings are not absurd,
But it's not truth if they didn't get the words
From the one they're hoping will hear aloud
Thoughts they made up, spilling into the crowd.

February 4, 2020
Susan A Brooke

Passion

I am a writer. It is what I've been given to do,
I'm older now, and perhaps, a little wiser too.
Finding my way over the past couple years
Took lots of practice and many with fears;
Some with missteps and some days with vales of tears.
And people thinking I'm so wet behind the ears.

Let the naysayers say, the unbelievers think
With God at the helm, I'll be a poet before you blink.

Many people can rhyme a line or two,
But I write poetry usually out of the blue.

Given to me, minds whirling for sure,
God's got this new work, it's his to secure.

February 13, 2020
Happy Birthday, Mom
Susan A Brooke

Moving On

The way seems a bit rocky,
There's no real solid ground.
Moving forward's so hard,
When there's none like you near or 'round.
You step, you falter, you fall back again,
That old way was safer, a zone you believed in.
Up you go, get on your feet.
The new you is waiting, there's a new street.
Take your time, don't let others rush
All the time you need, tell others to hush.
This is your new life, the old such a bore,
Your new life, though someone's keeping score
Of how many times you will fall back in,
How many times the enemy will watch you sin.
This way, though rocky, is much safer for sure.
Heaven's angels were singing, that was your allure.
Your eternity is chosen, you'll be there soon;
But first, walk this journey with God - he's your new fortune.

February 13, 2020
Happy Birthday, Mom
Susan A Brooke

Trust

What really can you say? When it'ss lost, it all goes away.
Some still want to try once again,
Believing their person, it didn't mean what it meant.
Time and again you hold to the lie
That your love didn't mean it, so again you try.
Like Mom and Dad who are there to protect,
But live their lives in ways that yours becomes wrecked.

Trust hurts and is hard to see,
When everyone around was sowing a seed.
Back-stabbing, name-calling, beatings, and more
Quickly and painfully shut trust's door.

There's only one way to regain the trust,
Asking forgiveness and change of heart a must.

Does it really matter at all to you?
If not, you'll live your life all askew.

February 14th, 2020
Susan A Brooke

Longing

Can be described as intense desire;
Snug, warm, cuddled up by the fire.
When you don't have what you think you want,
Your heart's mind plays tricks when others flaunt
Their happiness, security, and loving ways
In your face, unaware how it plays
Out in your mind, you being alone.
No love to come, to call your own.

Longing is a gift from God,
Written in His word a path I trod.
Perhaps I'm not a soul yet set free
From past life experiences, and need to be
Free so that my heart will flutter
At your love without all the clutter.
Yes, loneliness and longing go hand in hand
And sometimes loneliness plays in the band
Called marriage or courtship, one never knows;
How being together comes with life's blows.

So much to say, but today's not the day;
Rather I'll focus on loving and Happy Heart's Day!

February 14, 2020
Susan A Brooke

Truth

Hurt's so painful you won't see
What the truth is, doesn't belong to me.
Tearing your soul, you cry to your end
Waiting for God a new truth to send.

Will you see it, accept what he's said?
Or will you deny it, knowing what's in your head?
Heart feelings can sting like a wasp.
Knowing your truth you cannot grasp.

Head knowledge now seems so secure.
Head knowledge lies to you, holds you oh-so-sure
You're in the right, the ways made sure
In your mind, there's no other detour.

Take out the fight, the need to be right,
Put in the love, what a beautiful sight.
God's truth is unconditionally loved.
No matter your path, you're his beloved.

Truth, once painful, is no longer the allure.
God's truth in love, becomes your cure.
Forgiving all, down to the last crumb,
Begins to free you from feeling so numb.
Don't let your truth be the one you see.
Accept God's truth, live life, be free.

February 22, 2020
Susan A Brooke

Darkening Lenses (Covid Begins)

Loneliness

Loneliness still sits in my core,
Longing for what? Believing there's more.
Some kind of love I thought I once knew,
But now I know the difference - that love was skewed.
Though part of twosome, that quickly became lies,
When that wrong love forgot how to try.
To stay a couple, to fight for the end
Of a life well-lived with your best friend.
When there's no life lived laughing, crying with friends,
The life once lived is hard to comprehend.
Why does this happen, God? Why so alone?
Am I really that bad a friend no one will phone?
Asking me to join them, in whatever ways -
Games, cards, bingo, movies, dinner, or plays.
I've prayed, I've pleaded, I've begged God and still,
I'm still all alone here, waiting for him to fill
The deep longing of loss I feel.
No family or friends with whom I can steal
A few moments' time for laughter or fun
Or crying together over movies, so undone.
Please, God, I'm begging again, once more,
Fill my cup, Lord, with friends and family galore.
Maybe even a companion for days and nights' allures.

February 22, 2020
Susan A Brooke

Snow

Cold drops, fluffy, icy, heavy, wet, dry, flies!
These words speak of something I myself despise.

Can't sing of it, love it, or want it around,
Makes me feel caged, stuck indoors, homebound.

Of course I can get out, walk the grounds,
Driving in it's another thing, think I'll stay 'round.

Snow carries pitfalls of hurts.
People, cars, SUVs, and trucks are the worst!
Freezing, no warmth, waiting in fear and then…
May you be found 'fore untimely things set in.

Do I like the thought of snow?
Simply said: "A BIG FAT NO!!"

February 22, 2020
Susan A Brooke

Chance

Chance, or luck, in my life just can't be found.
Others have the luck of the draw, in their life it comes 'round.
If words were luck, I have the witches' brew,
If words were luck, I'd be a billionaire too!

My luck exists with the words on the page.
Perhaps by chance, this work will be "All the Rage!"

One day, my words of poetic strands
Will be bought by many in every land.

My words are what I offer now,
Hoping one day to take the bow
On stage where other's gifts are seen.
These words on the page will brightly gleam.

Gifted words, once hidden from view,
Released by God's healing, they're coming through.

February 22, 2020
Susan A Brooke

Poetic Words
(Before the Pandemic)

These words of poetry are all mine
Written during the tests of time.
Words become light and life,
Giving, faith-renewed, written without strife.

February 22, 2020
Susan A Brooke

Kisses

Life's feelings, mind reeling;
About love, about death.
Kissed as one takes one's last breath.

Tender, warm, soft, placed with care,
Urgent, needy, longing to still be there.

Sexual tension, release the spheres,
Caught in your mind, brings on the tears.

Cuddly, fuzzy, warm baby snuggles
Make laughter come - baby struggles
Against the cheek, the ear, any place,
Anywhere you plant a kiss on their face.

Kisses, deep feelings, intense
Want to let go, this love makes sense.
Till kisses kissed feel foreign and staid,
These kisses of love are now betrayed.

February 22, 2020
Susan A Brooke

Winter

Dull, dark, gray, icy, cold, depressing, no life, all is dead;
Slow, not caring, bleak, freezes, snow slippery, daily dread.

Slumps, worry, shut in, no fun, depressing; died a little more;
No outs, stuck, brain mush, help, freezing rain, cried a little more.

Out, Out, Out! Want out of this pit,
Stop the crap from coming down,
Put out the SUN,
Get rid of this pith!

Days upon days of dark, depressive clouds
Spitting out snow, ice, sleet, like its proud;
It's got you stuck in, depressed, mad,
Angry as a hornet's nest.
Give it up already!
Give us a break, Winter, give us and the clouds a REST!

February 22, 2020
Susan A Brooke

Possibilities

Oh, what a day I've had.
Is this for real, or am I going mad?

Much joy and encouragement in the morning's meet
With a sweet lady I vowed to greet.
After years with no contact or spending time,
Reconnection breezily passed like rhymes

Then quickly home to pet the cats,
Feed them so there's no repast.
Onto the next one, this one's hard,
Giving a friend a hand without regard

Notes she must know to help her grow
And help her loved one follow the road.
A path that's been set, that could lead to despair,
But with help from friends and God above,
Help us all, Lord, be aware.

February 24, 2020
Susan A Brooke

Not Today

Unmotivated, the writing's not coming forth.
Past several days have given no worth.
No words to the page, experiencing no due.
Alas, ahh me, what shall I do?
Trying the words on for size,
Are they lying to us, a false oblige?
They're really not coming through my mind.
I'm feeling bereft, no words, so unkind.
Amazingly, I've written these words down.
A laugh for the night, tomorrow will come 'round.
A new day for a new start and words to the page,
I'll see that it happens, no excuses to stage.

Susan A Brooke
February 26, 20

Lost

Been lost inside my life this week.

No real time for creating, so to speak.

It can be said I've been busy, for sure,

Meetings with business friends, life team, friends, not premature.

Needing my soul time, I spent time with my Lord,

Not neglecting my time in His Word.

So yes, I was lost, and yet I was fine,

Meetings, friends, Jesus, and all was aligned.

Susan A Brooke
February 29, 2020
(LEAP Day)

Envious Strife

(Been trying to write this one for a while. It's been stuck in my
head; no words would come…until today.)

We've spoken, I made apology, and you're still holding on
To something from my life, for yesterday playing Satan's pawn.
One would have thought the past was gone, long dead,
As holding on to perceptions should no longer be spread.
But today you proved by the words of your mouth
You can't let it go, your prayer was too far south.
Calling it "speaking boldly" like all would know,
Or I should be afraid of it and off I'd go.
NOPE, not happening, God still pulled me in,
I'm serving with the others, unafraid of your sin.
You've got something to deal with, oh, you who's fooled so many,
It's not my baggage to deal with, it's yours a-plenty.
I circled around, apologized, prayed and more.
Gave it all the Lord, he washed it from shore.
On my behalf, the shore's washed clean,
On yours, my dear ex-friend, shows worry it seems.
I'm not jealous, angry, envious, or worse,
God's time with me took it all, 'twas his verse!
He's promised to change it, make it all anew,
I took him at his word, gave it up, now it's all on you!

Now?

My day began again with delay,
NO motivation for at home stays.
Doing things regular and mundane
Makes these days sometimes profane.
Other things I'm trying to ignore,
Like taxes, cleaning closets, to be sure.
Though all needing to be done,
I think Spring has literally Sprung!
Wanting to spend time outdoors
Doing things more exciting, a whole lot more!
Than being stuck inside on wintry days,
Made me so depressed, needless to say.
Couldn't motivate myself much to care
Tried telling myself it was too much to bear.
So now I'm in a bit of a quandary,
With real things needing to be done,
But I want to be outside in the fresh air,
Finding all things FUN!

Susan A Brooke
March 2, 2020
(Before the Pandemic hit)

Today

So here I am with computer, paper, and more,

Sitting here diligently striving to score,

A poem, a thought, and good words today

All taking up my desire to go play.

Not all days can be play days, I know.

I'm wiser than that, work comes first, needs to show.

I'm really wanting to score in the biz land,

Starting a business with my helping hands.

So much to do, a plan, print, place, and then,

With God's instrumental help, I'll know when.

Others contact me for some dearly needed help,

Calling on me as I get reviews from Yelp.

This, this, is what I'm to do;

Not tied down, like gum to someone's shoe.

This is me, freely helping as I should.

My gifts and talents used as I could

Be of a great help with someone's little chore,

To me and to them, though, it's so much more!

SA Brooke
March 2, 2020

(On starting my personal assistant business, before the nasty pandemic ruined so many lives.)

No Words?

I have not a word today.
Turn my head a certain way.
My neck and ears make it sway
Inside my brain so I can't stay
Here, making poems up this day.

I despise being lame and ill;
I despise being made to sit still.
I know God slows us down for a reason,
But this has been my entire season
Of life, for the past couple of years.
I don't want no more, no more fears
Of sicknesses coming about again.
I've had my share, give to others when
Their wonderful lives are all gaga and fun.
Let them sit down through the seasons of sun!

Susan A Brooke
March 8,2020
(Did I have COVID then?)

Age, Is It Just a Number?

Good grief, I lament, I'm feeling so old.
How did I get here? I'm not that bold.
Daughter of mine will turn twenty-nine.
Ouch! That hurts my ears, it's not sublime.
Read a letter from a government agency too,
Said if I was sixty-six, I'd have NO penalty drew
For working more and making the bucks.
That would cause my taxes to take a flux.
Though I'm feeling older now after all this,
Can't wait for the next year, I can earn all I want
Without a hit or a miss!

SA Brooke
March 9, 2020

Taxes

Today was not a day to relax.
Today was filled with Fed and State tax.
I prayed before I started and
Asked God to come into the mix.
Sure glad I did – 'twas long and arduous
But I'm OK with what I got, I didn't have to nix
Any of the time or brain muscles spent.
Though four-plus hours was hard, it carefully went
Right for today, without the frustrations before
Asking God to the party, could not have done more.
Years in the past, when I'd groan and cry,
Complaining I can't do this, why do they make me try?
Tax companies have been more helpful, it seems,
As people don't want foreign preparers by lien.
So use their apps, following their leads.
Ask God to join and do your own frustration-free.
Rainy, gray Monday, first day of the week.
Jump ahead "by the clock," a day you'll want to sleep.

S A Brooke
March 9, 2020
(Still not feeling well. Reflecting back, it was probably Covid-19.)

Darkness Extolled

Isolation
A COVID-19 RESPONSE

Isolation is one thing,
For me, self-imposed.
But to be made to isolate
Goes against grain and code.

Wash your hands,
Look presentable -
Who even dares?
There's no one to see,
Nowhere to go,
NO ONE EVEN CARES.

Susan A Brooke
March 20, 2020

Not Scared

Like a ticking time bomb
My heart beating on the pillow where I lay
Boom boom, boom boom, boom boom
My mind screams of future disarray.

A day when all will be silent
No need for hearts to beat again.
The shell of my existence left,
Just lying how it began.

Life without life, but no slap to wake,
Instead my soul was God's to take.

Dismal, drear, this poem is, I fear
But don't care cause its making my head clear.

From all the doom and gloom being wrought
By COVID-19 and the people's thoughts

It's not rain that's holding us back,
It's people's lives being taken, that's a fact.

Susan A Brooke
March 21, 2020
(Pandemic closing in)

Spoof Quarantine?

So you thought fourteen days quarantine was unfair?
Try thirty, says the government, we'll see how you fare.
Living under ultraviolet lights with no sun and fresh air
Doesn't even give a thought to the eyes as they glare.
They're glazed and you're stuck, like a honey bee to its comb,
Serving with the queen bee, the ruler of their home.
I was once the all-knowing queen,
Now I'm an old crone, or so it seems.
Not quite young, not quite old,
Stuck in the middle, like ages of gold.
Remember them while you can, the days will become long.
Do the countdown each day, begin with a song.
A song of praise even though you're stuck,
A song of praise you don't do luck.
Praying daily to the God above
Is the only way through, assured of His love.
End it sooner than later, and we'll all resume
Lives lived in a rush, all gone too soon.
Savor your time, a gift from above.
Teach your kids patience, showered with love.
Can thirty days extra be the time we need?
Please, God, I'm afraid, mental health will exceed
And come on some others with undue speed.
Onto the canvas of this thing we call life.
Due to being shut in and the government strife
Ruining our lives because they're so full of fear.
We have to obey, even though we know you're near.
Some of the country's following KC's suit.
Give us the break at thirty days, show us the proof.

That's all we needed to get this under control,
While you lead us in the march, your light to extol.

Susan A Brooke
March 22, 2020
(More COVID-19 time)

Canvas of Life???

Onto the canvas of what we call life
Due to the shut in and government strife.
Running our lives because they're so full of fear.
We have to obey even though we know you're near.
Some of the country is following suit,
Give us a break, at thirty days proof.
That's all that's needed to get this virus under control
While you lead us in the march, your light to extol.

SA Brooke
3/22/20
(Pandemic just declared eleven days ago in USA)

(Hahaha! It's October 13 now. No END in sight. It's still out there. Lies still being told, fear still being mongered. People are so DONE and so WEARY of this. It's still forced isolation - stay apart! Wear your filthy masks! Can we please get a reprieve on this crap? Wash your hands, use sanitizer. The last two are "DUH!")

Pandemic Day #95347+

April 3, 2020

Contemplating life's current unknowns;

It occurs to me Jesus died all alone.

His father turned, forsook him as Son,

And we can't be with loved ones when life's day is done.

Crying, pleading. Father, don't you see?

It's your only begotten son Jesus, why you forsaking me?

My son, oh, my heart, I'm crying for you;

I just can't go back on my word to only save you.

I'm dying inside with each breath you no longer take.

I'm dying inside you, we're still One for love's sake.

I can't describe the pain, oh, I cry, how it hurts!

To make you be alone because of earth's curse.

You're dying, my Son, is not all for naught,

Though my tears I just can't seem to stop.

Your life for others that is what is TRUE.

You'll see one day, Son, it's life I'm giving anew.

One for the many billions and more,

Give your life to my Son to even the score.

Resurrection Day this year will come and go,

How many will heed the call, add to the flow?

Don't pass on without Jesus as your only hope,

Dying without him is like having no rope

To hang onto in this day of uncertain times.

Just let Him love you, ask him into your lives.

He didn't die on the tree so a slave we would be,

No, He died on the Cross to save you, a life set free!

Looking for the End of This!

I'm so tired of hearing words about the virus.
God's Word to us, he requires of us
To trust in him, when the way seems drear.
Trust in Him, he'll make the way clear.
Not what you think or want him to,
But in His time, he'll surely come through.
I'm done with all your DOOM and GLOOM.
God, help me to hear and in my heart make room
For words of love, encouragement, and security
For I'm with you, regardless of the severity.
This illness came, this illness will go.
You know all about it, your hand you'll show.
When it's time for all to see your hand
It'll cover the earth, it will span each land.
No doubt here, then God really showed up,
Though I have had my moments, I saw an empty cup.
Then all will see, though many still will doubt,
But that will be on them, I'm going OUT with a SHOUT!

S A Brooke
April 7, 2020
(More Pandemic time at home)

Time Stands Still

Don't you know, haven't you heard?
There's a thing in the air, so absurd.
Causes an illness, but not to be feared,
Cover your mouth, don't touch your face, so weird.
Just a few months ago, laughing, joking, and hugging
Now everyone's acting like their neighbors are mugging.
Not just your neighbors, but family as well.
Doesn't matter if in the same house you dwell.
Orders issued, stay at your home.
Only go for necessities, order on the phone.
Only essentials workers may dare
To go out, go to work, come home, maybe scared.
No churches, no movies, inside or out.
Can't claim God told you to meet, you've got no clout.
No schools, most over the net is done.
Home schooling for all has taken new meaning for some.
No play on playgrounds, shoot hoops, picnic for fear -
Nope! Stay six feet away and keep germs from loved ones near.
You'll likely survive, the recovery rate's grand,
But some would rather be alone with their head in the sand.
No meetups with friends unless you do it online.
No meetups for traveling, life's so very unkind.
The few stores that are open are for food and gas.
No parties, clothes, shoes and other boarded up, alas.
No haircuts, salons, nails done, look like a bum.
Unless you're a politician, rules don't pertain to some.
Trained in those arts? Are you able to fulfill
Their lives with culture of the current swill?
No museums, plays, symphonies, concerts, and more.

Just STAY in your house, don't go out past that door.
Funerals are live-streamed, families left alone,
Unable to grieve their loved ones passing, can't even atone.
The words been given, time is to be measured at home.
The longer the better be grounded alone.
WHO wants to take children from loved ones? There's fervor
While one in the house is dealing with being a survivor.
Separation anxiety is killing far more
Than COVID-19 ever hopes to ensure.
Yes, today the world is standing still.
God? Are you listening? Is this really your will?
That some should perish without hearing your name?
Your word doesn't support that, that's not your claim.
II Timothy says you want no man to perish
So all who do from this had your word to cherish?
We'll never know if they were your child or a fool,
Not on this sick earth, their choice, was that cruel?
The choice they made to believe in your hope
Was hopefully chosen 'fore they had to cope
With this sickness and then lost thought of you, God,
And ended up at life's end with a life so odd?
They didn't walk with you, but perhaps at the last,
Their final words were to you "I confess."
I'm a sinner. I need you, oh God, please save me
To fulfill your promise, Father, to let none go free
Of their own accord without making the choice
To become one of yours, with their last voice.
Oh, Father, I pray your word to be true,
That all that have perished had heard of you.
It was their choice to make, mine only to tell
Of a wonderful love, a place His son made me to dwell.
Not only in this house where I'm grounded,

But with you, Father in heaven, where I'm surrounded
By your loving light that will take me home
To live with you forever, oh Lord Jesus, come!

Susan A Brooke
April 7, 2020
(More COVID stuck at home time)

Tabouleh Rhasa Phobia

Fear of the blank page. April and May 2020
Fear of the fear mongering pandemic lies being told.
Fear that my anger is springing up again
Fear that I will forever be alone. Isolationism at its best!

What Is Wrong with You?

What the heck is wrong with you?
Banging on the walls at 4:45.
Do you think I'm still trying to scare you?
I've got my own life to live, be alive.

You're a doped-up oldie who thinks she's queen
To the corner of the world where your duplex is seen.
Lord, give me grace to pray for her when
She's constantly irritating my life and then,

My brother comes by to do some work, they're his, it's what he does.
So then she gets haughtier and worse-acting. To her he's shown no love.

No compassion or hello, but he's busy, you see
But she doesn't care, for she thinks she's queen bee.

Hateful, spiteful, the demons in her abound,
But my God is bigger, shut her mouth, her body, no more to pound.

Since my God's bigger and I'm more healed inside than seen
I prayed the Authority Prayer over the house, yard, garage, and the
queen.

SA Brooke
May 22,2020
(Crazed Neighbor Episode No.???)

Small Hope

I had a small hope, a glimmer if you will,
That love would come to me in life again
Like the soft wafting of a warm summer breeze
Like the unconditional love of a newborn child
Like the tree waiting to bring forth its blossoms in spring,
Like the first chilled air of a cold winter snow.
Waiting, expectantly, but alas, no such love was to be had.
Like the lone cry of a lonely whip-poor-will
Whose spirit is crushed by no response
From a female looking for a mate.
Like a branch crushed by the foot
Like a toy in two pieces a child dropped
Like a candy split in two, but never shared.
The heart is a fickle thing,
Broken upon the least little denial of hope.

S A Brooke
May 20, 2020
(Alone again, in my car in the closed park. Pandemic mess!)

Life is Fair...Not!

Oh, little children, be very aware,
Life isn't ever, not ever fair.
The devil decided so long ago
That we'd all be hurting, 'twas his goal.
For the depths of the pit called hell,
He determined life just would not go well.
For anyone of any age, strife will strike like a balloon popped in
your face,
Illnesses, cancers of bone, body, and brains,
Blood and tissues, lungs is his game.
He let it all out, the human man to destroy,
He doesn't want God to win, our sins he'll employ.
So watch yourself, little one, teen, or elder,
The devil awaits to make life helter-skelter.
Ensure you're on the right path with God and the Son.
Get them into your life, so this war can be won.
Not by you, but by the one who is so fair.
One day he's returning, coming back in the air.
But in the meantime, you can fight the spiritual war
By prayer, meditation, and so much more.
Give your life to the One
Give your life to the Risen Son!

SA Brooke
May 23, 2020

(Sitting alone in my car at the closed park. STUPID PANDEMIC!)

My Babies' Lament

Why did you give those babies still unknown
To someone whose life's seeds were yet unknown?
When you knew you would only take them back
From someone who's life was a total hack.

I knew so little, was ignorant of life so much,
I couldn't handle another's life as such.
Pre-destined was what I believed,
So I guess I don't understand why there was so little reprieve?
For their lives and mine, I was too afraid and so,
I gave them back to you, which you already know.

Do they stay babies or did they grow into beautiful people that I
won't know?
I don't know that I've ever heard that asked. I guess that's a new
question for me, a task.

I can only say I'm sorry, dear ones, for letting go of you
I knew God would take better care than I ever could do.

But did I cut your life short?
Will others be mad?
Who either lost babies or
Ones couldn't be had?

Took a long time to get me to this place
Where I could write truths, while others to face;

Turn theirs away, truth they can't handle and put in a vase;
But I'm forgiving myself, I'm in a much quieter space.

S A Brooke
June 8, 2020

The Project

Don't know why this has taken so long to get underway again.
Struggling with what to say and how and finding a way to begin.
Knowing I'd be triggered was a lot of what was on my mind,
But only telling part of the story didn't seem so kind.

Without knowing the basis of thoughts and actions taken,
One can only guess why someone's soul and life was so shaken.
For my mind, that left too much up to the imagination,
And many know to lead a group's thoughts makes a wearying nation.

Though not all is told, it couldn't possibly be
The book would be too long and readers tiring of it easily.

There's no conceptualization like the book *The Shack*.
It's straightforward and condensed to bring out the facts.

Facts as I lived them, not you or your friends.
Facts as I felt them, living them to the end.

S A Brooke
June 20, 2020
(Trying to write the book too)

Bugs, I Detest Them!

Why did you create them, Oh Lord?
Trying to enjoy nature makes me hate them more.

Always in my face, on my body and then
Boom, one of them bites, stings, or BUGS, like only they can.

Had to resist being outside due to feeling sick
But I'm trying now to enjoy the morning with six candle wicks
Of citronella to burn away the allure
Of the bugs to my scent, I must be so pure.

No matter what's sprayed, scented, or not
They still come upon me like a bullet to a shot.

Fake spray, natural spray, or nothing as well
Drive the bugs to my side like I'm their holy swell.

Wind used to help, but no, it's of no help today.
Why won't the wasps, flies, little biters, and spiders just go away?

S A Brooke
June 20, 2020
(At friend's lake house)

Clarity

Walking early in the morning
Trying to clear my head
Making plans for big changes
No more moving dread.
Waking in this place
With the broken-down deck
And the broken-down neighbor
Who keeps giving me HECK!
Get a new job to add to the stream
Of income needed to make it, it seems.
So enjoying life I can continue to endure
Without all the minutia, the neighbor's manure.
Let her have HER place. I'm done with this fall.
They can let new neighbors have it, give them the ball!
I'm done, I'm making plans, I'm moving on.
May not be a large house, but God's got this one.
Can't count on others to help solve the row,
Only count on God to soften the blows.
Am I giving up? Yes, I can't live life like I can't.
I'm much more alive, jovial, a spirited aunt.
Goodbye, mean neighbor, Satan's spawn,
Find someone else to lie about the crap on your lawn.

S A Brooke
July 12, 2020

(After I was served with extortion and lies documents.)

Tribute to Shirley
End of life 7/13/20

Where have you gone, my dear sweet friend,
At the end of your journey, at breath's last end?

Jesus called, you're there with him.
This isn't a joke, nor merely a whim.

You lived your life as a daughter should.
God's loving daughter was your greater good.

Sweet, loving, caring, smiling for sure,
Your life was fulfilled, your love was pure.

Letting others know their life needed to be more,
You left every way open to enter through that door.

Your love of your family, your church, your God -
That's the volumes being spoken for your enter into nod.

You're safely home now, back in the Father's arms.
Out of life's dangers here, out of life's harms.

S A Brooke
July 14, 2020

(On the passing of dear, sweet Shirley Peters. Amid all this COVID crap, racial tension, and fear-mongering, she was a trooper for the cause of Christ.)

Remember or Forget

How do I remember how to forget
The things in my past, no more to fret?

I thought this idea up while chatting with you,
But you're part of my past, so what do I do?

Can I be selective and forget all the wrongs,
Or will I forever be reminded of ills so strong?

I don't want the horrible memories always popping up.
Each time we connect, don't want it crowding my cup.

I think we may have a special connection going on here.
Is it a worthy one God, or should I continue to fear?

Being stuck in the past because of what I remembered of them,
Or can I really move past and begin again?

S A Brooke
July 14, 2020
(Conversation with a high school memory)

Beyond Pain

Though some talk of days of sweet little activities happening,
Like games of hide and seek in the dark
Or playing it while covering two square blocks
Or roller skating
Or your mom calling you in for supper when it got dark
Or playing kick the can outside till ten or eleven PM
Or running through the sprinklers with your swimsuit on
Or the smell of bacon frying in the pan on the campfire.
Those are a few of my good memories.
But mostly my days waved over, filled with an ache -
An ache that goes beyond human comprehension.
Sitting alone in the grass looking for four-leaf clovers
Am I seeking the luck of the Irish or
Desperately seeking love and attention?
The right kind of love, not the negative kind,
From old boyfriends, parents, and siblings.

S A Brooke
July 21, 2020

Another Time, Perhaps

I haven't been able to write.
My life, oh, what's happened to life?
Lockdowns, viruses, hate crimes, and more
Got me thinking this country's at war.

We're all angry, sick, protesting with ire.
Some are even setting this world on fire.

Not for the right reasons, but to gain
Attention, the wrong side, the left, while choosing to maim.

Looks the other way, now enhances it thrice,
But where's the conservative right? Looking away twice.

This year's important, I get that, most do.
But to look away and not stop the hatred makes most of us blue.

Blue as in sad, not changing party lines.
Dear Lord, help us all, we are not doing fine!

S A Brooke
August 8, 2020

Lighten the Path Again, Hope Endures

Determinded Death

Breaking free, oh yea! For me,
I've been shackled here too long.

Broke free of the desire holding me down.
Now I feel freer, able to move on.

Not playing in the playground of the place where
My desire caused imminent death.
Only playing in the playground of the good and righteous,
The place where life is breath.

Breath of the spirit, who's been dealing with me.
Waiting on me to finally see
That the death needed to happen.
No more sensual desires.
And now I know to play in the playground
Set up with Holy fire!
By my Father, the Son, and the Spirit of Life
No more striving - I'm giving up that unholy strife.

S A Brooke
August 10, 2020

Isaiah 54:10 "My kindness, my peace, shall not be taken away."

Taboulah Rasah
(FEAR OF THE BLANK PAGE)

Taboulah Rasah is for real
Starring down this blank page is a big deal.

Should have stopped for something to eat.
This hunger kept at bay is no easy feat.

I've been stuck for quite a while, I'd say.
Not afraid, just unsure of what's at stake.

Plunge forward, take the leap.
Your Father's got this, no need to creep.

Write the epilogue, prologue too.
Get the book formatted, he'll publish it for you.

Rejections aren't kind and so expected,
But there's someone waiting, with breath abated.

Waiting for what you have to say
In word and poetry, make their day.

It'll be to your delight
Move forward without fear, without fright.

This said, after being stuck for months,
COVID pandemic cramped everyone's fronts.

September 11, 2020
Always Remember 9/11
S A Brooke

False Hope

Is false hope a lost hope,
Or one that can be regained?
Is false hope a lost hope,
Or one that's now profaned?

False hope is hard to bear.
It wears you down, takes a lot to care.

Your sprits soar, thoughts are high,
Only to be dashed on stones again, makes you cry.

Up again, down again, up again once more,
Down to the depths of the pit you're thrown, your thoughts die,
poor.

You never want to hope again, You never want to try,
The enemy's got you despondent. You can't even shed tears to cry.

Anger evolves, pounding fists, all be damned.
Never to care, not once, never ever again!!

September 11, 2020
Always Remember 9/11
S A Brooke
(Seven months into this pandemic crap!)

Gathering Soon – Covid Be Damned!

We're gathering from near and far,
Finally seeing each other's stars.

Oh, how we've missed the love of a few.
Though we can't hug, we'll still be true.
True to the love of one another,
Created for community, like no other.

Wonder what the animals and birds would do
If God commanded them to not congregate too?

Is it something we're likely to find?
Nope! It's just us sheeple whose life is unkind.

Oh Lord, when will it end?
I need my hugs, Lord, friend to friend.

September 11, 2020
Always Remember 9/11
S A Brooke
(Seven months into Covid crap!)

Purposeful Pain

What purpose, what truth
Lies within the Pain?
Isolation, sickness, mental exhaustion,
Loneliness is there to gain?
Who do you see sitting all alone?
What thoughts are they forming?
How does your heart feel seeing the pain?
Each tear cried from the unknown storming.
Doubts and fear rage within the noise in the mind.
Who can quell and silence it?
Silence begins as each doomsday finds a way,
Looming larger and larger, bit by bit.
Still no answer, no help for the pain.
What is required of one feeling so low?
To be freed indefinitely would begin,
But no, each must suffer, the Word says so.
He hears each one as we cry, beg and plead,
We feel it fall around us as night.
He was the one who took time to bleed.
Is he really as deaf as one thinks, 'tis might?
All knowing, seeing, being, and feeling,
He cries when we cry, saving each tear in a bottle .
How does he continue to carry more pain
Without the fleeting thoughts of being throttled?

S A Brooke
Sept 21, 2020
(We're still in the COVID mess.)

Love Is Not Ugly

Haikus - I could write a hundred a day
But poetry fulfilling is not easy to say.

Many ways to write what's in that big heart's hole,
Many ways to read the completion of your soul.

Misunderstood? Oh, to be sure,
It'll happen, like the words, so not pure.
Tried to explain the love unknown,
'Twas skewed around, was soiled, met with frowns.

But pure feelings, can they be conveyed
Without others thinking it a false array?

Not likely, so its misunderstood,
Agape love, unspoken, wholly loved, for good.

I could write the sonnet to be sung,
But my head in shame I'd hung.
They've taken what you meant to me,
My God, loving father-figure, and made it be
Ugly, twisted, tainted, so foreign, unknown,
Now leaves me feeling bereft, alone.

Not my place to make them see,
Your Godly, fatherly love was necessary.
God knows my heart, to our faith I'll be true,
God knows your heart, and how my healing needed you.

Your help reminds me of *The Shack* a lot.
God showed himself in ways that Mac understood and got.

No boundaries taken in God's delight,
To show pure fatherly love to a not-young sprite.

Papa, mama, Father, brother, friend,
Godly love surely knows NO END.

September 11, 2020
Always Remember 9/11
S A Brooke

The Five Haikus of September

Eagle
Eagle flies above
It always knows its way round
Every single day.

Home
Eagles fly above
It always knows its way home
Each time its flying.

Prettiest
Red bird, blue bird, finch
The yellow bird is pretty
Grass, tree, dusty ground.

Tree
Tree standing, not straight
Weathered, winds, rains beating hard
Lightning, tree falls down.

Sounds
Silence, pure, deafening, quiet
All sound, if you listen well
Tiptoes, like a mouse.

September 11, 2020
Always Remember 9/11
S A Brooke

Spoof Covid?

It wasn't a spoof, yet it's gone on far too long.
Is it political? You betcha - some trying to sing their song.

Force them all home, make them broke, then you'll see
How much you make sheep of people like these.

Mandate this and mandate that, and oh, be sure to wash those hands.
Don't touch this, wash as soon as home, but let me touch your card
in this land.

Half-truths everywhere, but do you see?
They're not saying the virus is not real, but not of such horrified quantity.

Laying blame's the easy way to get out of a joke,
Who cares what happens to you, I'm still getting paid, you bloke.

By all your tax dollars and more
Gifts by the hundreds, so much allure.

Sheeple got taken for a ride, it seems,
On the merry-go-round of a political heat.

When, God, when does this end?
Will November 4 be the turning point? Will help you send?

Yes, it's likely some patterns of life had to change.
But do we all have to live differently, make such drastic change?

S A Brooke
Sept 21, 2020

Not Really the Last Poem

Today I'm writing the book's last poem for sure.
For the book to be compiled, oh, how I endured.

It's for more than just me, who's needed to write.
No, it's for all the other who lived life in strife.

Healing rains came. Lord, how they hurt,
But you were always ready to stop the bloody spurt.

Tears cried, many words spoken in sorrow.
Never thought I'd be on this side of tomorrow.

There was so much anger and the hidden before.
Would I ever forgive, let go, stop holding this store
House of pain, of hurts and regrets
For a life of choices not made? I was their pet.

Few saw it from that distant shore
Where I was forced to live among the poor.
No cries heard, no compassion shaken
Over the little girl's innocence taken.

Ah, life, 'twas then, but not what is now.
God's holy hands on me, heading the bow.

Longings, desires, there's still quite a few,
But I know who's got me. I am secure.

Not earthly love, but from heaven on high.
Though an earthly love? Is it still a desire?
Sharing life with one who can stand beside
The once-innocent child who's heart bled and died?

S A Brooke
Sept 21, 2020

Truly Last, But Not the Least

Contemplations begin with the morning's break.
Pears in oatmeal…yeah, not so great.
Pain in the crown from six weeks past
Still makes me wince hard, hoping this won't last.

The reason for this poem was clear.
I'd never really written for friends so dear,
Or family that tries to include me now
As children grown, go on from bow to bow.

My family, as I'm inclined to say,
Tell me I'm welcome most any day.
They too have their limits and times,
Not always on the ready of a dime.

Their care and concern and even love is known.
Others despise the comfort I'm shown
From spending time with family galore,
But also sweeter, quiet times and more.

Sweet friends, oh, I rue the day
When COVID came and ruined our ways
Of just hanging freely, laughing too hard,
Or in quiet contemplation when we're being scarred.

LORD, bless them all, quiet friend, family, or foe
Your Love, LORD, sees us all through the frough*,

We're all unique, but made for your refrain,
Keep us healthy, joyous, till you come again.

S A Brooke
October 6, 2020
(For the last poem of my first book of poetry.)

*Frough: brittle or fragile, like our current daily lives due to covid,
racial tensions, election year…

The Angry One

Why are you so angry?
What has hurt you so bad?
That every day you walk about
Slamming everything, your face so MAD!

I've been hurt exponentially too,
Yet I'm not always angry.
I wonder what's happened to you?
That seems like all your life is so sandry*?

Your extreme emotions in your eyes
Gives way to one who questions why.
What are you always so angry about?
You've nothing to smile for, give a happy shout?

I know why I, when angered still,
Can stop the anger and change the course.
I have the best of everything inside.
It's what's keeping me from screaming full force.

It's so hard being nasty every day.
Every minute, every hour, but that's your way.
Why, why, don't you give in and let it go?
Give all your grief to the God, he's got this. So…

Why the ugly grimace? Why slam the doors?
Reminds of words said from long before.
Your face will freeze if you keep looking that way.
Why do you want anger when peace can sway

More friends than scowls ever could.
Change the look on your face like you know you should.

Begin then, live life, with a differing look.
Begin to feel joy without all the strife.
I'm praying for her, Lord, every night.
Now she's a challenge to help conform her life.

Help her, LORD.
Help her to see,
The only way is
With you to Be!

S A Brooke
October 9, 2020

*Sandry: extreme

The Epilogue

Ten-four, good buddy! Isn't that the sign off for someone leaving a conversation?

I am officially leaving this conversation piece. I have other poetry to write, of that I am sure. God and his Spirit are always putting words and thoughts into my head and heart that I hear and don't always write down. So, I'm sure there are more that God alone is reading from my heart. And there are others that will be written and amazingly poured into a book that will flourish and be read like other authors in the family have been (i.e.: Rupert Brooke, an English poet.).

To say that this book was a long time in coming is an understatement. Eleven long years from when I first started counseling and sending the pastor copies of my poetry (Which, by the way, most have not been included either as I cannot locate them any longer. He put them in storage after he moved.).

I do feel compelled to state that this week brought about even more forgiveness. Things I held onto in my heart that weren't yet revealed to me when I thought I had forgiven everyone in counseling. God works that way, you know. He won't always give you what you think you need when you think you want it. Ofttimes, he gives it to us at a later date, and usually as a "oh, my gosh" moment. This finally makes sense to me! Here's an example: I hated driving the freeways. I get it, freeway means you get to go faster and get there presumably sooner than you planned. So, I moved from Wisconsin to Missouri to take a job downtown to force myself to learn to drive the freeways. Well, that in and of itself is a big, fat joke. Everyone knows that the freeways take way longer in rush hour traffic. But learn to drive them, I did. For some reason, though, I always felt disgusted and angered and hated it when traffic was stopped and I could not go anywhere. There was no escape. Then, all of a sudden, it hit me like a ton of bricks (Thankfully not a real ton of bricks as that would have smashed the car and my head!). But there I sat with this sudden revelation! Being stuck on the freeway was a big-time trigger to me. It was a constant reminder of all the times I was abused as a child and under the control of my abuser, with no way out. With no way to escape. Absolutely nowhere to go, no way to move, no way to stop what was being perpetrated against me. Then traffic moved, and I was able to breathe again and move freely again, but with a sense of dread still attached. That was because I knew the possibility of it happening again, just as it had in my early years of life, was still prevalent. Does that make sense to you?

There are many things that may trigger us, but if we are not looking for God to help us with them and help us work through them, we lose out. We won't hear from him or his Spirit. I try to be more conscious these days but still find myself sometimes realizing something hours or even days later. Yes, I play those scenes over in my mind till I get what I need from whatever the situation or circumstance was, and some of them might involve an area of forgiveness. Forgiving others; forgiving self; forgiving God. Yes, I said forgiving God. Waaay too many of us hold onto things in our past with a perceived idea that we have forgiven everyone, but we forget that we need to ask forgiveness for the anger we feel at God. Anger because we feel he let us be in this place; anger because he didn't give us what we wanted; anger because we had to suffer a loss; you name it…then think about it… deep within your soul…don't rationalize it or try to justify your thoughts and feelings. But deeeeeep within your soul, your true self, what do you need to forgive someone, yourself, or God for?

That's mostly my testimony. Learning to forgive. Not forgetting, because I want to be prepared when someone else may hurt me with the same thing, but true forgiveness.

Focus on your insides and evaluate what God is doing in you. God wants you to have an experience with him for this season that FAR EXCEEDS what you expect!

Ok, God! I heard you! I am expecting a great experience with you through this season and with this book. I AM DARING TO DREAM BEYOND ALL MY EXPECTATIONS! And I am being FEARLESSLY AUTHENTIC.

This is MY story. Not my family's. Not my friends'. Not yours!!! These were my experiences. My remembrances. Oh, how funny. My word for the year 2020 was "Remember." No, it is not a coincidence. There are no coincidences with God. My word for 2021 is "Connect." If I can connect with one person who sees some of their life in these poems and makes a change for the better, forgiving others, forgiving themselves, forgiving God, then this eleven-year journey will be worth it.

Ahhh……"BUT GOD……!!!"

Ephesians 3:20-21a "Now unto him that is able to do exceedingly abundantly above all that we ask or think, according to the power that worketh in us; unto him be glory……" (KJV)*

Much love,
And not the end…
Tequila Rose

Aka: Susan A. Brooke/SAB
And affectionately by my former work team as "Essay"

"The Faces of Shame"

Author Unknown

I FEEL LIKE A TREE WHO HAS BEEN DEFILED

A SLENDER BIRCH WHO HAD BEEN STRIPPED OF ITS
BARK. MY TRUNK HAS BECOME A DARTBOARD FOR
THE ARCHER. INSCRIBED IN MY SPINE IS THE WORD
SHAME.
MY LIMBS HAVE BEEN TWISTED. THEY HANG BY MY SIDE.
THE SAP HAS BEEN DRAINED FROM MY PUNCTURED
VEINS. MY LARNYX IS RUINED; I CANNOT SCREAM.
THE BIRDS OF THE AIR ARE AWED BY THEIR VISION.
THE DEER CANNOT WATCH.
THE SQUIRRELS BURY THEIR HEADS.

EVEN THE RODENTS RUN FROM THE SIGHT. THE SKY
LOOKS AWAY.
THE SUN LOOKS AWAY.

AND THE BLACKNESS REMAINS.